IF FOUND PLEASE RETURN TO:

👤 _____

✉ _____
  _____

📱 _____

Greater Than a Tourist Book Series
Reviews from Readers

I think the series is wonderful and beneficial for tourists to get information before visiting the city.

-Seckin Zumbul, Izmir Turkey

I am a world traveler who has read many trip guides but this one really made a difference for me. I would call it a heartfelt creation of a local guide expert instead of just a guide.

-Susy, Isla Holbox, Mexico

New to the area like me, this is a must have!

-Joe, Bloomington, USA

This is a good series that gets down to it when looking for things to do at your destination without having to read a novel for just a few ideas.

-Rachel, Monterey, USA

Good information to have to plan my trip to this destination.

-Pennie Farrell, Mexico

Great ideas for a port day.

-Mary Martin USA

Aptly titled, you won't just be a tourist after reading this book. You'll be greater than a tourist!

-Alan Warner, Grand Rapids, USA

Even though I only have three days to spend in San Miguel in an upcoming visit, I will use the author's suggestions to guide some of my time there. An easy read - with chapters named to guide me in directions I want to go.

 -Robert Catapano, USA

Great insights from a local perspective! Useful information and a very good value!

 -Sarah, USA

This series provides an in-depth experience through the eyes of a local. Reading these series will help you to travel the city in with confidence and it'll make your journey a unique one.

-Andrew Teoh, Ipoh, Malaysia

GREATER THAN A TOURIST- BOQUETE CHIRIQUÍ PROVINCE PANAMÁ

50 Travel Tips from a Local

Shelley Audette Settles

Cover designed by: Ivana Stamenkovic
Cover Image:
https://commons.wikimedia.org/wiki/File:Boquete_Panama_(27211038742).jpg
By dronepicr (Boquete Panama) [CC BY 2.0
(https://creativecommons.org/licenses/by/2.0)], via Wikimedia Commons

CZYK Publishing Since 2011.
Greater Than a Tourist
Visit our website at www.GreaterThanaTourist.com

Lock Haven, PA
All rights reserved.

ISBN: 9781724107138

>TOURIST

50 TRAVEL TIPS FROM A LOCAL

BOOK DESCRIPTION

Are you excited about planning your next trip?

Do you want to try something new?

Would you like some guidance from a local?

If you answered yes to any of these questions, then this Greater Than a Tourist book is for you.

Greater Than a Tourist - Boquete, Panamá by Shelley Audette Settles offers the inside scoop on the highland community-turned expat haven, Boquete. Most travel books tell you how to travel like a tourist. Although there is nothing wrong with that, as part of the Greater Than a Tourist series, this book will give you travel tips from someone who has lived at your next travel destination.

In these pages, you will discover advice that will help you throughout your stay. This book will not tell you exact addresses or store hours but instead will give you excitement and knowledge from a local that you may not find in other smaller print travel books.

Travel like a local. Slow down, stay in one place, and get to know the people and the culture. By the time you finish this book, you will be eager and prepared to travel to your next destination.

TABLE OF CONTENTS

DEDICATION

This book is dedicated to our wonderful families, especially our amazing children and grandchildren. They may not always understand our wanderlust, but they still love us, accept us and support us in our choices.

ABOUT THE AUTHOR

Why did Shelley and her husband Ken choose Panamá when they left the states on New Years Eve 2016? Shelley explains: "We'd both visited Russia and the Philippines, as well as several countries in Central America. We'd tasted what it was like elsewhere and Panamá ticked several boxes for us. They have a solid infrastructure with Internet reliability and a strong expat community in this hemisphere. Plus, we knew that a sister/daughter of some of our Costa Rican friends lived in Boquete. All these factors made Boquete an easy decision, and an easier transition for us to make this our first, long-term foray into living abroad."

Shelley is an Air Force veteran, Christian minister, teacher and freelance writer who provides sales copywriting and web writing for business clients throughout the world.   She is an active member of Boquete Authors Group and is currently researching and writing two books in the religion genre. In what little spare time she has, she enjoys exploring the area and playing cards with her friends.

An international traveller and adventurer by nature, Shelley is probably the only licensed, ordained, motorcycling-riding grandma to have ridden her Suzuki VStrom from New Mexico to Panamá alongside her husband riding his Kawasaki Voyager. That's another book worth of stories, about the beauty of Guatemala to being swindled in El Salvador… and the fascinating people they met along the way.

HOW TO USE THIS BOOK

The Greater Than a Tourist book series was written by someone who has lived in an area for over three months. The goal of this book is to help travelers either dream or experience different locations by providing opinions from a local. The author has made suggestions based on their own experiences. Please do your own research before traveling to the area in case the suggested places are unavailable.

FROM THE PUBLISHER

Traveling can be one of the most important parts of a person's life. The anticipation and memories that you have are some of the best. As a publisher of the Greater Than a Tourist book series, as well as the popular 50 Things to Know book series, we strive to help you learn about new places, spark your imagination, and inspire you. Wherever you are and whatever you do I wish you safe, fun, and inspiring travel.

Lisa Rusczyk Ed. D.
CZYK Publishing

OUR STORY

Traveling is a passion of the "Greater than a Tourist" series creator. Lisa studied abroad in college, and for their honeymoon Lisa and her husband toured Europe. During her travels to Malta, an older man tried to give her some advice based on his own experience living on the island since he was a young boy. She was not sure if she should talk to the stranger but was interested in his advice. When traveling to some places she was wary to talk to locals because she was afraid that they weren't being genuine. Through her travels, Lisa learned how much locals had to share with tourists. Lisa created the "Greater Than a Tourist" book series to help connect people with locals. A topic that locals are very passionate about sharing.

WELCOME TO
> TOURIST

INTRODUCTION

*"The earth has music for those
who listen."*

--William Shakespeare

People who come to Boquete, Panamá, seem to
have an easier time tapping into the earth's music.
There is a rhythm and majesty to the mountains, the
cloud forests, the rivers and the waterfalls.
Somehow, in a cacophony of birdsong and howler
monkeys, you find peace. You can be one with
nature here, even if just for a few days. Clear your
head, regain perspective, and 'have your senses put
together' as John Borroughs, a naturalist and activist
in the U.S. conservation movement, wrote.

Indeed, in this place called 'plenty of fish' or
Panamá, there remains unspoiled vistas and pristine
air. Caressed by ocean on either side, adventure lies
within.

*"The world is a book and those
who do not travel read only one
page."*

– Augustine of Hippo

1. WHEN TO VISIT

Boquete is beautiful all year. Our 'dry season happens to correlate to winter in the States, so that's when most part-time Canadian and American expats come to Panamá. Of course, Boquete welcomes guests all year and Europeans visit regularly. The rainy season here winds up as 'winter' starts, with the weather being ideal through April. More people are here during these months so expect prices to be a little higher.

Rainy season can be hard to gauge. Often, the weather is gorgeous during the morning with showers coming for a few hours every afternoon. Other days it might rain all day, or not at all. It's a way of life here so no one seems to mind. You'll still see locals out walking where they need to go.

2. GETTING HERE

If you are flying in, you will go through customs at Tocumen International Airport (PTY) in Panama City. But from there you have options. One option is to fly on to Aeropuerto Internacional Enrique Malek (the airport in David, the capital of Chiriquí province) down the road about 45 minutes from Boquete. For a

15

surprisingly short 45-minute flight, it can be expensive to add this leg of the trip onto your ticket from the states. You might get a better rate buying a ticket from PTY to David separately. Try to price it both ways. There are three flights with Copa airlines daily back and forth between David and Panama City.

An alternative, once you land at Tocumen, is to go to Albrook Mall bus terminal and take a bus to David. Then transfer to a bus headed for Boquete. You'll get to see more of the beautiful country this way.

Don't be put off by bus travel. These buses are very comfortable, safe, reliable and run frequently. The air conditioning works full blast so you might be cold unless you bring a jacket. If you decide to take a bus, you can take the "expresos" (overnight express bus). You'll sacrifice seeing the scenery but it will be a lot cheaper than flying.

Locals almost always travel by bus between Boquete and 'Panamá,' which is what they call Panama City. Panama City is large and cosmopolitan. It can be easy to forget another Panamá exists in the rest of the country.

3. UBER IN PANAMA CITY

If you want to check out the Miraflores Locks of the Panama Canal or Casco Viejo in Panama City before or after your visit to Boquete, I highly recommend using Uber instead of a taxi. Download the app, set up an account and give it a try if you haven't already. You can even pay an a tad extra for an English-speaking driver, but don't expect fluency.

Unlike a taxi, with Uber you will know the price ahead of time and everything is charged to the credit card on file. You don't need to carry extra cash. There's a record of who picks you up and they have incentive to get you where you want to go quickly. Taxi drivers have been known to overcharge tourists or take the long way around just to increase their fares.

The only problem we have ever had using Uber in Panama City is when we didn't get downstairs to the hotel lobby fast enough after calling. Our Uber driver was hassled and driven off by taxi drivers in front of our hotel. Taxis drivers here hate Uber, but Uber is clearly a better choice here.

Unfortunately, Uber is not an option outside Panama City.

4. CURRENCY

Immersing yourself in a different culture for a week or two is fun and exciting. But converting currency in your head while negotiating with a local, can be tricky. No worries - Panamá adopted the US dollar in 1904 as their legal currency. Bear in mind, when you pay for items you may get change back in a combination of dollars and cents or balboas, the Panamanian $1 coin, and smaller Panamanian coins.

The Balboa (which they call a Martinelli here) is a strikingly beautiful, two-metal amalgamated coin about the size of a quarter but you won't mistake it for one. Conversely, their fifty-cent piece is large like a U.S. dollar coin. Use either currency freely here, but remember all Panamanian money converts to 'cheap souvenirs' once you return to the States.

Speaking of cash or 'en efectivo' as they say here, you can easily find ATMs at local bank branches, unlike in some other Central American countries. Fees are a bit high so you might as well draw out what you think you'll need to make the ATM fee worth it. Don't plan on using your credit cards. You might be able to use them but you might not. Some grocery stores, gas stations and restaurants take them now but not all do, so it's better to plan to use cash.

5. PHONES AND APPS

Anytime you travel out of the country you have to make some decisions about your phone. You can buy a cheap phone in country… we did that for a 10-day trip to the Philippines, based on some advice we'd received. Bad advice. We constantly had to load more minutes and it cost us much more than it should have. (Anyone want to buy a used phone you can only use in the Philippines?)

If you have a smartphone, make sure you can "unlock" your phone and use it with another service provider. Then determine what kind of SIM card it requires and whether your phone will work in either GSM or CDMA cell networks. If it doesn't have that capability and you need a new phone anyway, get one in your home country before coming to Panamá. Phones are expensive here.

We purchased my Iphone in the States to use it with Verizon and they use CDMA technology. We verified before I bought it that it has a small door on the side that allows me to pop out the Verizon CDMA card and install a different SIM card from my cell service provider in Panamá. (If you want a bit of free trivia so you can amaze your friends, try to remember that SIM stands for Subscriber Identity Module.)

We stayed in Panamá City for a week when we first arrived. We went immediately to a cell phone company's outlet at the Albrook Mall to get new SIM cards. Knowing more Spanish in Panama City certainly would have helped but we managed to purchase what we needed by showing the lady behind the counter what we wanted.

If you are visiting Boquete, get a SIM card with Claró or Movíl. They both provide decent coverage in this area. Use the 'pay as you go' option. Get the minutes and data you think you'll need during your time in Panamá. If you run out, you can buy 'reload cards' in stores everywhere. Insert your new SIM card into your phone and restart your phone. (Make sure you store your U.S. SIM card in a safe, protected place to pop back in when you return.)

For us, the cost was less than $5 initially for the SIM card, then we pay $15 a month for 150 minutes and 4 gb data. You probably won't need that much; we rarely use it all. Many Panamanians only load $5 at a time on their phone.

Everyone uses What's App here for texting and free phone service. That's the cheapest way to go since your hostel or hotel likely has Internet available. You can load What's App in the States before you leave.

If you travel much abroad and expect to have WiFi, consider putting Skype and/or MagicJack on your phone. We have both. I work with clients in the U.S. and they call my Washington state 'home' number. It rings on my cell phone and 'land line' here in Boquete. We opted for a multi-year deal, which got us their equipment inexpensively. We now have free calls to and from our friends and family in the States. We could call using What's App too, but many of our friends and family in the States don't use it yet.

As for other Apps, that depends on what you want to do here. If you plan on birding, you might prefer a digital Panamá Birds Field Guide app with bird sounds included, to a printed guide.

6. PACKING FOR ALMOST PERFECT WEATHER

A while back some Boquete promoters advertised our little community as the one place in the world with perfect weather and no natural disasters. That's almost right. Boquete's 3900-foot elevation means our weather is extremely mild compared to the rest of hot and humid Panamá. The country lies below and to the west of the Hurricane Belt. But we are situated at the base of Panamá's largest mountain, a volcano. Scientists tell us the volcano last erupted around 1550 and shows no current signs of waking, but technically the volcano is not dormant. We feel an occasional mild tremor originating from elsewhere…from Costa Rica or Nicaragua, or even the ocean depths. Earthquakes do not concern the locals.

During your visit to Boquete, you'll enjoy 'springtime' temperatures, usually 20 degrees or more cooler than in the rest of Panamá. Our balmy weather rarely registers above 80 or below 70 degrees Fahrenheit. Depending on when you visit, you may even want a sweater or light jacket, especially after the sun sets. Certainly bring something warmer if you plan to hike or to jeep to the top of Volcan Barú.

Due to our proximity to the equator, we see little variance to our weather or hours of daylight. We enjoy about 12 ½ hours of daylight no matter what month it is. We frequently have light breezes and a fine mist that reminds me of an Oregon beach's coastal mist. It's called "bajareque," or "ba ha ricky."

As I previously stated, our rainy season is roughly May to December and a 'dry season' December through April. It's green and beautiful here because we live on the edge of a tropical rain forest, locally referred to as cloud forest. Bring a rain poncho and perhaps a compact umbrella.

The country itself is between 7 and 10 degrees from the equator. Even if it appears overcast, the sun is closer overhead and its UV rays are stronger. Bring, and use, a good sunscreen unless you plan to buy one here.

7. SENSE OF DIRECTION

Panamá is a southwest to northeast facing country (contrary to the rest of Latin America which is 'down' from the U.S.). Somehow this plays havoc on people's natural sense of direction. Yes, the sun still rises in the East and sets in the West, but it's easy to get turned around here.   Oddly, since Panamá itself makes an S-curve, ships that are headed west transit the Canal towards the east. Ships that are heading east, transit the canal headed west. It sounds crazy, but check a map.

8. HOW TO GET AROUND

The locals walk, take taxis or buses, and even ride horses.

Buses are interesting. You have the regular buses, which are newer and quite comfortable. Then you have local 'chicken' buses or 'colectivos.' Up until recently you could spot these older school buses a mile away. They were gaudily bright with exquisite, hand-painted murals on all sides. Flashing lights and streamers dangled from every imaginable exterior place. One bus might glorify the late, great Elvis and another exotic animals. These decorations became extensions of each driver's personality and friendly one-upmanship.

They earned the U.S. nickname 'chicken buses' because they are cheap local transportation favored by poor farmers who occasionally might use one to haul smaller livestock in the outlying areas. The government tried to outlaw these buses in Panamá City a while ago when we arrived, but were without success. They remain too important to the locals and to the economy. However, the government did successfully regulate how these buses could be adorned. Now you will no longer see the distracting streamers and the flashing disco lights. The amazing paint jobs with murals remain.

In addition to riding buses or using taxis to get around, you can rent a vehicle next to the airport in David, or perhaps lease one from the used car dealership in Boquete. I don't necessarily recommend either unless you have 'white knuckle' driving experience and get full insurance. Taxis are a good choice here, and you will likely share the ride with other passengers.

If you are athletically inclined and have come to sample our biodiversity and outdoor adventures, you might consider renting a bicycle or a scooter. The hills around here would require a mountain bike and sturdy legs but cycling is a growing sport here.

Habla Ya, a popular Spanish immersion school here, also runs a number of eco-tours in the area. They rent mountain bikes, helmets and camping gear. Their students even get discounts (if you come to learn Spanish.) They do not rent scooters but I understand you can rent scooters from a few of the fincas (farms), like Finca Lerida, and through Boquete Mountain Safari Tours.

9. TIPS ON WALKING

People walk in Boquete because it's compact enough to do so, because parking is limited, and because many locals don't own cars. However, the terrain is un-level, and walkways often have holes or obstructions. When you walk, watch where you step and try not to be distracted by the sights.

We don't have crosswalks and stoplights in Boquete so forget about 'jaywalking.' Cross the street carefully looking both ways, and do not cross in front of the first stopped car at a corner. It might seem like crossing between two stopped cars is dangerous. However, locals consider this safer than crossing in front of the first stopped car at an intersection.

They know the driver has his eyes on oncoming traffic, looking for a sizeable gap in which to pullout. The driver will pull out into traffic when he can, likely without looking to see if a pedestrian is trying to cross. However, if you walk behind the lead car, before the next car in line, that second driver will see you. He can't move forward yet anyway until the lead car pulls out.

10. NO STREET ADDRESSES

You might think U.S. influence in Panamá from years of building and managing the Panamá Canal would extend to other infrastructure conveniences like street addresses, but not so. Panamanians do not have mail service to their homes and you won't find many addresses on properties. Occasionally there are named street signs, just don't count on it.

You can get to your hostel or to a specific restaurant simply by telling your taxi driver name of the hostel or restaurant you want. To get to a friend's house, refer to a landmark such as Plaza San Francisco or Ivan's in Alto Boquete. Tell the taxi driver you want to go to 'a street across from Plaza San Francisco, before you get to Ivan's.'

11. MIRADOR

One of the first stops you should make when you arrive in Boquete is the tourism bureau on the bluff overlooking the town in the valley. It's a big, yellow, two-story building next to the colorful Boquete sign you can't miss. If they are open, you can pick up trip brochures from tour groups and visit with the attendant for suggestions, like you would any tourism

27

office. Buy a cup of Kotowa coffee there; Kotowa is one of many coffee 'fincas' that offer coffee tours.

Not to worry if neither Kotowa or the Tourism Bureau is open… You really stopped for the 'mirador' – the beautiful overlook of the Boquete Valley. Walk past the shrine on the left toward the bluff to the side of the building for an iconic view of Boquete.

12. SPANISH OR ENGLISH?

If you want to brush up on your Spanish, you'll have ample opportunity in Boquete but keep in mind pronunciation here has more similarities to Caribbean Spanish than to Latin American Spanish. A few words may also be different from the Spanish you took in high school.

A derivative of 'beaucoup' borrowed from the French, is the word 'buco' and here it means 'a lot' or 'much.' 'Blanco' naturally means 'white' or 'blank,' but it also means 'cigarette.' 'Gallo' still means rooster but it can also mean 'cheap.' Forget saying 'adios' when you want to say 'goodbye.' Say 'ciao' instead like the Italians do.

Elsewhere 'yo' (the word for I) sounds like 'yo' but here they pronounce it with a harder sound, more like 'jo.' Panamanians also tend to aspirate their 's' at the end of a syllable or word. For example, the Spanish word for 'waterfall' is 'cascada.' Elsewhere, cascada would be pronounced 'kas-kada' or 'kas-katha' (soft d, almost a 'th' sound). Yet here, the 's' tends to become 'h' so the word you hear sounds more like 'kah-kada.'

No worries if you don't know Spanish. It's okay to speak English in Boquete. Expats from Canada and the U.S. have lived in Boquete for years, which means a number of locals have picked up at least a little English. Menus often include Spanish on one side and English on the other. The staff at restaurants favored by expats and those who work in tourism trades are usually bi-lingual. If they aren't, you can often get a bystander to help translate for you if you find you need help.

13. TWO TYPES OF LOCALS

One of the first things you will notice on the streets of Boquete are the indigenous Ngobe-Buglé people. (Technically, these are two different people groups but are often referred to just as Ngobe. You'll also see it spelled Ngäbe. Either way, it is pronounced nōbē with a soft 'b.'

You'll spot the women and young girls immediately in their ankle-length cotton dresses decorated with designs around the neckline, arms and waist. Ngobe men and boys dress plainly and would blend in better if it were not for the colorfully-dressed women with them.

The Ngobe-Buglé people remain the largest indigenous people group in Panamá and are said to be the only ones that were never conquered or even intimated by the Spanish conquistadors. Local Ngobe here now work almost exclusively as laborers on the coffee plantations. They keep to themselves unless they mingle to sell bags of handpicked dried beans and such. They speak Spanish and their own Ngäbere dialect, but often can't read or write, leaving their children who learn Spanish in schools to read and translate for them.

Panamanians on the other hand are extremely social. They will smile and greet you at with 'buenas' at a bare minimum. Buenas is short for buenas días (actually good morning, not good-day like you might think) or buenas tardes (good afternoon). 'Buenos' would be short for 'buenos noches' or 'good evening.' Avoid being rude by acknowledging them with 'buenas' or 'buenos' in return.

14. RECYCLE & REUSE

You wouldn't necessarily think 'recycle' would be a topic in a book like this. But one reason you'll love Panamá in general and Boquete in particular is that we have far less trash along the roadside (in most areas) than many other Latin American countries have. Perhaps it's the years of U.S. influence during Canal construction and oversight, or recognition of the importance of the eco-tourism dollar to Panamá, but they understand that trash hurts tourism. Cleaning up previous dumpsites comes a little slower but overall, Boquete is beautiful and free of the usual trash.

Now you can actually save cardboard, paper and aluminum to drop of at a local business-turned recycling center. Recycling is 'new' to Boquete; it wasn't an option we knew about when we first arrived. Hopefully, recycling household plastics and glass isn't far behind.

Stores have been phasing out plastic bags in favor of paper. Cutting down on non-biodegradable plastic bags is one of Panamá's goals, both to protect its stunning biodiversity and its ecology. It's easy to see the positive effect that reducing this kind of litter and eyesore has had on Panamá, and Boquete in particular, anytime you visit a less progressive country.

Go even 'greener' while you shop for your organic fruits and vegetables by bringing your own reusable, canvas shopping bags.

15. SECURITY

Boquete is quite safe as long as you use wisdom, like you should anywhere. I would not have any qualms about walking at night, other than needing to see well enough to navigate rough ground. They have police on bikes downtown whose main purpose is to keep the expats and visitors safe.

Panamá itself uses police at checkpoints throughout the country, specifically at certain points on major roads. Sometimes checkpoints pop up on side arteries so they can check for expired licenses, current passports and the like. Often they will ask to see everyone's identification, which should include your passport. Carry it with you in a safe place. You may be asked for your passport before booking a tour or using a bank; you just never know.

Rather than thinking negatively about the checkpoints, focus on the fact that they do seem to keep some negative elements away. The friends who took us under their wings when we first arrived explained to us that before the checkpoints, there used to be more problems with gangs and with other undesirables entering the area to burglarize homes. As Panamanian residents now, the regular checkpoint knows our car so we are almost always waved through.

16. WHERE TO STAY

Options appear limitless in Boquete even though it's a relatively small town of 20,000. Your budget really determines your options but the good news is that you do have great options in every price range. Many places will provide local, unique experiences.

Keep it inexpensive and try a hostel or a local hospedaje. You can stay in cabins by the river as we first did, or lodge at many of the coffee fincas, bed and breakfasts, or unique resorts in the area. If you are planning a longer stay, you might even find a short-term rental or house-sitting gig with a little effort. Many places will come fully furnished and stocked with kitchen items if they offer more than a bed and bath.

Throughout this book I mention some of your lodging options as they appear under other headings.

17. THE PANAMONTE

This historic hotel retreat with restaurant and two bars was once the premier resort in Boquete for diplomats, politicians and other elite business people who wanted to escape the heat and humidity in the rest of the country. Ingrid Bergman, Richard Nixon, Sean Connery and the Shah of Iran have all eaten or stayed there.

Over the last 20 years some its grandeur has been outstripped by others. Yet the Panamonte has reinvented itself to serve growing ecotourism interests. It remains a peaceful, quaint place to dine with friends on the expansive front porch, or watch the World Cup in one of its two bars.

18. TREE TREK ECO ADVENTURE PARK

In the hills north of Boquete, past homes and coffee farms, the paved road ends and becomes a set of laid concrete tracks just wide enough to balance vehicle tires on so they don't slip off into the rain-gouged, gravel ruts. If you've never been to Tree Trek, you might not think navigating this uncertain road, up the steep, winding hill is worth it. But it is.

35

High atop the mountain rests a world-class eco resort with hiking trails, bar and restaurant with a killer view, and cabins and rooms to rent. If you are a nature lover or birder, this would be a prime place to consider staying but you would likely spend all of your time here or invest considerably in taxis. They offer a canopy tour (also known as zip-lining), a Geisha coffee tour, a tea tour, a hanging bridges tour and a bird watching tour.

The canopy tour can be enjoyed by young and old alike, but you'll need a healthy back and the ability to jump up to hook your equipment onto cabling. Some stations require a little more 'jump' than others but attending guides will help. The Hanging Bridges Tour gives you an elevated perspective of the biodiversity of Panamá's tropical cloud forest. The walk includes a circuit with 6 suspension bridges and almost 3 miles through the treetops within the private forest reserve, Rio Cristal, located in the Talamanca Mountain Range. This range abuts the largest nature reserve in Central America and the UNESCO World Heritage Site, La Amistad International Park, situated half in Panamá and half in Costa Rica. The jungle park is largely unexplored.

If you don't have your own transportation, you can make reservations for any of their tours at Plaza Los

Establos on Central Avenue in the middle of town. Catch a jitney from the Plaza for the 20-minute ride to Tree Trek.

19. RIO ENCANTADO CALDERA

Just 15 minutes outside Boquete, situated on both banks of the Caldera river near the small village of Caldera, is the Eco Lodge and Nature Resort called El Rio Encantado (The Enchanted River). If you are a nature lover or birder, this is another prime place to consider staying. The area around El Rio Encantado was set aside years ago and protected from development. They have a tree house, cabins, groomed nature trails, a regular swimming pool and three tropical swimming holes in the nearby Caldera River. Most notable though is their centralized location to the Caldera hot springs. Caldera, by the way, means 'boiling' in Spanish. The advantage here over Tree Trek is transportation. You can easily catch a bus to and from Boquete from Caldera.

20. TINAMOU COTTAGE DELUXE JUNGLE LODGE

This place feels like remote jungle but it's in the hills, a mere 5 to 10 minutes east of Alto Boquete. Finca Habbus de Kwie offers coffee tours next to its 22 acres of private forest reserve, where they have three comfortable and romantic jungle cottages for rent. By staying here, you are close to all the wonderful restaurants and adventures Boquete has to offer yet you have privacy and seclusion. Your only real neighbors are monkeys and spectacular birds.

If Finca Habbus de Kwie sounds more Dutch than Spanish, it's because it is. Proprietors Terry and Hans van de Vooren immigrated here in 1998 and built the quaint lodges in the jungle to their exacting standards. They provide free WiFi in every cabin, home grown coffee, breakfast baskets and well-marked hiking trails. I'm not sure it gets better than relaxing on a private porch with no one around, surrounded only by the sights and sounds of nature close-up, sipping fresh Panamanian coffee.

21. FESTIVALS – FLOWERS, JAZZ & BLUES

Boquete, the sleepy little eco-community of 20,000, deserves its nickname as the 'Flower Capital of Panama.' Every January for 10 days the streets burst to host almost 145,000 visitors for the Flower and Coffee Festival that's been going on since 1984. Guests treat themselves to fabulous local coffee, indigenous art and handicrafts, and an epic showcase of bright colors, perfumed air and flower blooms everywhere. The Boquete Flower and Coffee Festival is family friendly with lots of entertainment options and games for the kids, food stands, beer gardens and more than 200 vendors. Sometimes this fairgrounds event is just called the Flower Festival, which is a shame since it isn't the only flower festival that calls Boquete home.

The Orchid Expo takes place every year at the end of March. The orchid is Panamá's national flower. This event draws thousands, far fewer visitors than the Flower Festival in January, but enthusiasts come from as far away as Japan to view the 500 or so orchids on display. The Orchid Expo's vibe is more subdued, graceful and academic, whereas January's

Flower and Coffee Festival bubbles with party energy.

Speaking of party energy, music lovers should check out the world-class Boquete Music and Arts Festival, formerly known as the

Jazz & Blues Festival. Touted by promoters as the 'biggest little festival in the world,' the Boquete Music Festival has about 16 different world-renown performers electrifying the air from multiple stages across the four-day affair. The whole town participates with art exhibits, garden parties, jam sessions and special events at participating restaurants. Even if you don't pop for expensive tickets to one of the stages during the festival to hear your favorite blues or jazz band, you can often catch them playing elsewhere in the local bar scene while they're in town.

22. TUESDAY MARKET AT THE BCP

Every Tuesday morning, rain or shine, the BCP hosts a food and souvenir market in and around the grounds. BCP stands for the Boquete Community Playhouse, a major events center in town. It's across the bridge from town center, near the fairgrounds, and is the only community theatre outside Panama City.

You can buy foodstuffs like fruits and vegetables, locally grown honey or coffee, pastries, breads and catered meals. Buy a bottle of kombucha and check out the Panamanian crafts, jewelry and blankets.

Once you've been in Boquete awhile, you no longer go to get a quick neck massage or a hand-carved, painted walking stick. You go to the Tuesday Market to see and be seen. It's where friends bump into each other and catch up on the week's happenings.

While you're at the Tuesday Market, you may want to pay a buck and take in the scheduled Tuesday Talk. You can hear any number of topics such as representatives from local clinics talk about accessing health care and insurance, chefs explaining how to select and prepare local foods or a discussion of local the flora and fauna. Come a bit early, the little community theatre only seats 100 and talks occasionally sell out.

Speaking of the BCP, check whether they happen to be doing a production while you're in town. One of the regular favorites is the Olde Tyme Radio Show, sort of a local talent show done in the style of classic old radio. Think of an off-off-off Broadway

production of "A Prairie Home Companion" and
you'll understand what fun it is. Regardless of the
scheduled musical or show, the BCP always puts on a
community treat.

23. FRESH FRUIT IN SEASON

Nothing beats local fruit. Here, yard fruit is papaya
and bananas, all year long!   I never thought I even
liked papaya because it tasted musky in the states.
Not so when the fruit is fresh; it's beyond delicious.
They have different varieties of bananas here and they
are more flavorful right off the tree than what you eat
in the states.

You can buy papayas, bananas, pineapples (piña)
and mangos, and other fruit in season at fruit and
vegetable stands throughout the community, or from
the back of a pickup parked along side the road.
Panamanians seem to prefer fruit a little riper than
what I consider optimal. So when I get papaya, I ask
them to pick one out for me 'para mañana' or 'for
tomorrow.' Most of the time, it will be just perfect
for eating today.

If you visit between June and August, you might
want to try guanabana, a.k.a. soursop.   Locals claim

this large artichoke-looking fruit has miraculous healing properties, able to blast parasites out of your body and shrink tumors. I don't know about that. Just wash your hands and slice it open as if you were preparing to carve a pumpkin. Scoop out the meat, separate the seeds from the slop and enjoy its tangy, sharp then sweet flavor. A little goes a long way.

If you visit during August/September, try Rambutan or 'Mamón Chino' (Chinese sucker). It's sold as a bouquet of small branches with prickly-looking yet 'soft to the touch' red fruit attached.

24. PANAMANIAN FOOD & OTHER OPTIONS

You'll find restaurant options for any kind of food you like here: steak and fish houses, Italian or Chinese. Or you can eat as American as it gets - burgers and beer. The interior communities of Panamá have an agricultural base so Panamanian food consists mainly of root vegetables, chicken, beans and rice. They do not eat many green vegetables and prefer fried foods over boiled. If you want to eat Panamanian food along with the locals, you can't beat El Sabroson across from town square. It's local food, cafeteria style, and items change daily.

Don't be surprised if you order a corn tortilla and you don't get the flat, saucer-sized tortilla you might expect. A Panamanian tortilla is a corn cake, a disk almost ½ inch thick and the size of a drink coaster. Tortillas are fried in oil and often come with a bland local white cheese that looks a little like feta but isn't.

Patacones (pat-ah-cone-es) are served with Panamanian food regularly. They are basically fried green plantains. My favorite way to eat plantains - by far - are plananitos. If you don't get plananitos at a restaurant, make sure you buy a bag at a store. Eat these salted, thinly-sliced fried plantains like potato chips. Warning: They can be habit-forming.

25. FRESAS MARYS AND SUGAR & SPICE

Fresas Marys and Sugar & Spice Restaurant often find their way into guidebooks and forums talking about Boquete. Sugar & Spice, with its world-class bakery and artisan breads, is on right side of the main road once you enter Boquete proper. You can't miss it. They have an apple pancake an inch thick and as large as your plate. Order this and you won't quickly forget it. (My husband and I ate there this morning... Guess what we ordered!)

Fresas Marys is for all things strawberry. It's a quaint little place decorated in cartoon strawberries that you also can't miss, as long as you know to turn onto Volcancito Road at the top of Alto Boquete before dropping into the valley of Bajo Boquete.

Personally, I think the strawberries here aren't quite as sweet and flavorful as they are in the states, so don't go to Fresas Marys believing the hype that your strawberry shake or sundae will be the best you've ever tasted. It will, however, likely be the best you can get here in Panamá and still very much worth the stop if you like strawberries.

26. COLIBRI AND IL PIANISTA

For finer dining, you have too many options to mention. One of my favorites is the restaurant at Tree Trek for their filet mignon. (I basically eat vegan these days but not at Tree Trek.) Another great option is the Colibri Restaurant on the way to Valle Escondido Resort Golf and Spa.

Colibri means hummingbird. The restaurant offers 'farm to table with a twist.' The multi-cultural couple who own and run it, Daniele and Carolina, focus on fine wine and fresh food from Chiriquí province, the pantry of Panamá. I'm not sure if it's their culturally inspired menu, which by the way somehow manages to please meat eaters, vegetarians and vegans alike, or the atmosphere, but I think you are sure to like Colibri. They even serve gluten-free options with panache!

If your budget won't stretch for Colibri, consider a hidden Italian food gem, Il Pianista. As others have said, Il Pianista looks a bit suspect from the outside. Park on the shoulder of the road and walk down a short slope to the stairs of this converted home. True, it is next to farm-worker housing and doesn't look like much. But driving by would be a mistake if you like great pizza, friendly service and wonderful ambiance.

Il Pianista is simply charming. Next to a gorgeous waterfall with flowers always in bloom, the restaurant even has outdoor lighting for romantic dining. This is a family business; the owners live upstairs like they would in the old country.

They serve authentic Sicilian food. Of course, you don't have to order the dish they are best known for: thin-crust, crispy pizza from their wood-fired oven. Equally delightful are their calzones and pastas. Portions are generous.

27. A PERFECT PAIR

Specialty coffee and artisanal chocolate – that's just what you'll find featured at A Perfect Pair Coffee Shop in a wonderful, two-story building downtown on a corner of Main Street. If they happen to be making chocolate when you visit, you can watch them through a big picture window.

The structure was built in the late 1800s when there were only 5 houses in town. Later in 1949, the property became the Monkey Bar. Now, upstairs in the lounge you can sip your locally grown coffee and munch on chocolate goodies. Visit with friends in overstuffed chairs, or compose your memoirs at a table on the veranda. You'll appreciate their fast WiFi almost as much as their delicious coffees and chocolates.

Boquete's version of Starbucks is definitely not on every corner.

They offer an impressive list of different coffees from 10 farms in the area, including the famed Geisha coffee. After deciding what coffee you want, you order it brewed using your preferred system: by German Chemex, by French Press, by Belgian Siphon or by Japanese V60 & Kalita. Each method has its advantages.

As I understand it, their chocolate comes from either Panamá or their farms in Belize. It is always first rate, melt-in-your-mouth delicious.

28. BOQUETE BREWING

My uncle used to brew his own beer and dark ales. If you appreciate craft beers more than beer bottled for the masses, then you certainly need to check out Boquete Brewing on the north end of Main Street. They'll be the first to tell you they are 'not a bar nor a restaurant.' They are a brewery with a taproom and a food truck. They play only rock music and have loud live music on the terrace during weekends.

There's no intrusive service, or service at all for that matter. You go up to the bar or the food truck and order what you want when you want it. What they do have is a great variety of 'righteous' craft brews, both ambers and reds, and a surprising amount of craft ciders and local rums as well.

Not sure what craft beer you'd like to try? Order a 3-beer 'sampler.' Just don't expect what they call "crappy corporate freezing lager beer" or "bland, wimpy-ass corporate light beer."

29. THE NIGHTLIFE

Boquete is not known for partying or nightlife, like Rio de Janeiro or Bangkok might be. Not even close. We have no shortage of great bars and restaurants; however, many spots are winding down by 11 p.m. Most bars close by midnight during the week and by 2:00 a.m. on weekends. During festivals and Panamanian holidays, they may close at 3:00 a.m. or even later.

Normal nightlife around town includes live music, karaoke hangouts and the local taproom. Locals hangout at Bar Coca Cola to dance salsa or merengue on the large dance floor. La Posada Boqueteña Restaurant has Latin dancing Saturday nights and many consider Zanzibar to be the best party lounge in town.

Occasionally you'll hear of parties at a waterfall or in one of Boquete's youth hostels, most likely Hostel Garden by Refugio del Rio. This is the same group hostel as Refugio del Rio, they just moved into new digs five minutes walk from town square. If you like the party scene, talk with bartenders around town, and hostels while you're here. This will put you in the right place to hear about a party if one's being planned.

30. NORIEGA FOR HISTORY BUFFS

All traces of strongman Manuel Noriega are mostly gone now. He died at age 83 in May 2017 of complications from brain surgery, after having served prison terms in the U.S., France and Panamá. He rose to power under General Omar Torrijos' 1968 military coup. Torrijos gave Noriega command of the military in David, just to the south of Boquete. Ultimately he made him chief of military intelligence, giving him the inside track to power. After Torrijos' airplane mysteriously blew up midair, Noriega basically controlled everything.

Noriega ruled Chiriquí province and Panamá with an iron fist as they say. Older locals remember him all too well because they lived in fear of him. Those were dark days in Panamá until the U.S. invaded and ousted Noriega in December 1989. If you can get the locals to talk about those years, they describe him as a 'very bad man' who had no problems assassinating rivals and taking whatever (or whomever) he wanted for private purposes.

He owned several properties in Panamá. His most notorious were a fortified seafront compound in Farallon, now the domain of vines and vandals, and

51

his party house in Chiriquí, where presidents and heads of states stayed. Noriega was a student of Japanese architecture which inspired the design of his mountain compound in El Banco, at the base of Volcan Barú not too far from Boquete.

Finca La Pagoda now belongs to gringo owners who remodeled it extensively. Writer Mark Heyer snagged a housewarming invitation to Finca La Pagoda from his friends, the new owners. According to Heyer, they found escape tunnels underneath the massive property and secret panels within it. One secret panel contained a safe with a human head inside. Speculation suggests the head belongs to none other than Hugo Spadafora. Dr. Spadafora was the outspoken critic who was detained and murdered in 1985 by Noriega's forces after he tried reentering Panamá on a bus from Costa Rica. His headless torso had been found stuffed in a postal bag after hours of unthinkable torture.

Of course, this 'update' regarding Finca La Pagoda is not part of any official record.

31. BOQUETE BEES HONEY TOUR

Even if you are squeamish about bees like my husband is, you'll love Boquete Bees's honey tasting (40 varieties), bee education, butterfly house with 35 different species, and coffee tour. Their farm is about a mile from downtown Boquete and very easy to find. They offer tours three times a day. Although I've heard of people just dropping by, I don't recommend it.

They want to teach people to see bees differently and to better understand how to care for our pollinators. They keep a wide variety of forage for bees, and offer different types of native bees to illustrate how bees and plants are meant to exist together. The bee tour is fascinating. Since the arrival of African bees, the honey industry obviously changed. All honey now comes from Africanized honeybees and they'll run a video explaining why they aren't on the tour. You will see examples of native stingless bees used by Mayans for honey before the Europeans imported honeybees.

Boquete Bees sells raw, minimally filtered honey. Some is infused with other flavors. Delicious. More than that though, their honey is pure and healthy, unlike other honeys from the developed world. This honey comes from wild plants with no chemicals. It's pristine. Their bees also are healthy. They don't use antibiotics or miticides on them.

Naturally, they approach coffee production the same way. They plant coffee bushes in a garden and tend to the plants individually. They don't treat them with any chemicals that can be harmful to bees or butterflies.

32. COFFEE TOURS

Visit Boquete and you will likely participate in our biggest cash crop in some way or another. This area sports some 1200 local coffee producers with Café Ruiz, the country's biggest specialty coffee producer, leading the pack. Seems like the world is just waking up to the fact that Panamá even grows coffee. This is certainly changing.

Take a coffee tour complete with tasting directly from a coffee plantation or finca, through an eco-tour organizer, or even through a local treasure like Boquete Bees or Tree Trek, both of which have coffee farms associated with them. It seems like everyone in the highlands around Boquete and Palmira grows coffee for personal use or export.

While all coffee grown in Panamá is slowing becoming world-renowned, the most exclusive and expensive coffee beans in the world come from a small handful of farms on Volcan Barú. A natural-process Geisha from the Lamastus Family Estates sold for $830 per pound at the Best of Panama Green Coffee Auction held on 8/28/2018 in Boquete by the Specialty Coffee Association of Panama. The record price paid for Geisha coffee the previous year had been $601 per pound, paid to Hacienda La Esmeralda of Boquete.

You can treat yourself to a cup of Geisha coffee here for half of what you'd pay in New York City. Affordable by the cup, you really ought to try this flowery, silky tea-like coffee while you're here. It's unlike any other coffee you will ever try, and you'll earn bragging rights among coffee aficionados.

Of course, you don't have to spring for a cup of Geisha coffee to enjoy Panamá's favorite dark brew. Relax at any Boquete coffee house with a great cup of local Arabica coffee.

Be sure to save room in your luggage on your return trip so you can take several bags of great

Panamanian coffee back home with you to savor or to give as gifts.

33. CHOCOLATE OR COCOA TOURS

What happens when a loving wife decides to handcraft - from scratch - an organic, Panamanian chocolate bar as a gift for her husband who loves quality dark chocolate? The answer: He falls in love with chocolate all over again so they buy and expand the local artisan chocolate business, Chox.

If you are a chocolate lover yourself, you can buy varieties of local Chox chocolate at the Tuesday market (to die for), stay at the Chocolate and Honey Hostel, and visit several different chocolate shops in town. But if you want to see how they make chocolate, and even make it yourself, then you simply must tour the 'homemade' Chox facility near Los Molinas, south of town. During high season, you'll see and participate in chocolate production from the point of winnowing the beans, following the chocolate recipe, right through to choosing your favorite chocolate truffle to make, then wrapping your finished candy. Yum.

Nina and Barış (pronounced Buddish) are chocolatiers crafting artisan chocolate treats from the fair trade cocoa beans they get from Bocas del Toro on the Caribbean side of the mountains. They also have relationships with several coffee growers in the area, and craft branded 'coffee-flavored' chocolate from each finca's specialty coffee roasts. Those chocolates are available for sale at participating coffee plantations when available.

I fell in love with Chox at the Tuesday market after I purchased a double-dipped coconut chocolate bar. I also sampled a milk chocolate nib and was blown away by the richness of its cocoa essence. This level of nuanced chocolate flavor is usually found only in dark chocolate outside of Panamá. According to Nina, I was noticing the amazing unique flavor of Panamá's premier cocoa beans, so unlike the bland mono-flavor of European chocolate made from African beans.

If making your own chocolate from scratch in Boquete is not enough, you can arrange a cocoa tour to the Bocas del Toro area where they grow fair trade cocoa beans in the Silico Creek community. Technically you'll be on the Ngobe comarca. You can taste the cocoa seeds directly from the tree and discover how they make chocolate from tree to

57

harvest, harvest to liquid, and liquid chocolate to finished product. It's tempting to overdo your chocolate fix at the end with a taste of fresh chocolate, traditional coconut Ngobe bread, and a cocoa drink.

34. RUM TOUR

Many Panamanians consider Carta Vieja 'the rum of Panama' but it's little known outside the country. The rum factory is in Alanje, Chiriquí, outside David. But with reservations, you can catch a tour from Boquete any Friday at noon. This is the easiest, tastiest way to learn about the history of sugar cane and rum production here. The name "Carta Vieja" means "old letter" and is said to originate from a recipe discovered in an old wooden chest by the company founder. Like many rum producers in Spanish-speaking countries, they use a century-old tradition called the Solera process to replicate its flavor in every bottle.

The Carta Veija Rum tasting and tour occurs at the factory about an hour's drive from Boquete. Tour organizers take care of everything including translation. Alternatively, you can contact Carta

Vieja Fábrica directly for a tour. This would be cheaper, but I'm not sure how well they handle English.

35. BIRD WATCHING AND BIRDING

Do you know the difference between bird watching and birding? I didn't. Bird-watching is what I do. Originally that meant me sitting in my recliner sipping coffee while hummingbirds frolic outside my window around feeders some four feet away. I have my binoculars and my Birds of Panamá booklet beside me. I've seen gorgeous male red-legged honeycreepers and Great Kiskadees. Birding is bird watching on steroids. True birders travel all over to stalk birds for the hopeful glimpse of them and record their finds on a growing list of seen species. Boquete is a paradise for both, famed the world-over.

Stay in Boquete very long and the mystique of seeing exotic birds grows on you. I saw large green parrots chattering up a storm in a tree across from a restaurant just this weekend. The thrill was undeniable.

Several groups do birding tours in the area but two stand out: Boquete Outdoor Adventures and Jason Lara Tours. Both have knowledgeable guides that speak excellent English, and both have telescopes to help you see the birds 'up close and personal.' Guides from both outfits recognize native birdcalls and know where to find the birds you're hoping to see. Both are also likely show you more than just some of the 220 species of birds that call this area home. On a bird watching tour you are likely to see brilliant orange and black butterflies and perhaps a rare, Nero Glasswinged butterfly. You might even see a sloth or two.

Of course, the usual goal of birders and bird watchers is to spot the legendary Resplendent Long-tailed Quetzal, one of the most beautiful birds in the world. It lives at high altitudes around the cloud forests surrounding Boquete. March and April are nesting months. Even if you don't happen to see a Quetzal, your guide will likely point out wrens, finches, white-tailed hawks, and of course, more fabulous hummingbirds.

If you don't want a formal tour, pick up a guidebook on the local birds of Panamá and head out on your own to any of the many hiking trails around Boquete and Chiriquí province. You may be able to spot fiery-billed aracaris, orange-bellied trogons, and orange-collared manakins. Or even green parrots like I did without even trying.

36. JUNGLE DE PANAMÁ WILDLIFE REFUGE

Dorothy and her rescued menagerie may quickly wrap themselves around your heart, just like spider monkey Deisy kept wrapping her tail around my leg. You'll find Jungla de Panamá located 10 minutes outside Boquete in Palmira.   They care for dozens of indigenous animals that find their way to them one way or another.

Owner Dorothy loves to talk about the animals she cares for, how they came to Jungla, and what happened to them. One of her owls was found without a beak…she surmises that he collided with a tree. She glued the beak back on and nursed him back to health. He looks like he's ready to return to the wild, even though he ate hamburger from my fingers. But he'll never survive on his own. His beak is operational but not strong enough.

It's important to note that Jungla is not a zoo… her goal is not to keep animals but to care for them until they can return to the wild if it's possible. A bit before our visit, she had just released several animals so we missed seeing a boa constrictor and some other animals. But a hawk she'd nurtured did some 'flybys' to say hello during our visit. Dorothy cares for both exotic and domesticated animals. A blind pony, friendly raccoon, two monkeys and many of her curious birds are permanent residents.

Before opening Jungle de Panamá about nine years ago, Dorothy ran an animal rescue in the states. She came here to 'retire' but my bet is she'll never say 'no' to an animal that needs a helping hand. Jungla de Panamá wildlife sanctuary is a wonderful educational environment. They host buses, special education students, and nature lovers of all kinds and all ages. Open daily, but you'll want to call first to inquire about current admission prices, the best time to visit and even volunteer opportunities.

Jungla de Panama also offers a restaurant where you can sing karaoke, a hostel and a casita for guests.

37. RACQUEL'S ARK

Returning from Bocas del Toro one day while my sister was visiting, we rounded a corner to find a truck stopped in the middle of the road. A sloth was crossing and yes, they are very slow! We got out of our vehicles and stood there two feet away as he made his final movements to the side. He was drenched from the previous rain but otherwise magnificent, and seemed as curious about us as we of him.

I can' promise you something this extraordinary if you visit Panamá, but if you don't see sloths and monkeys up-close and personal during your hikes, you can always visit Raquel's Ark. It helps to be in Volcán for some other reason, like seeing Sitio Barriles, but soon a new road between Boquete and Volcán will make the trip much shorter.

They accept donations and I suggest you call first since this is her private residence as well. At the current time, Racquel hosts a 17-yr old Jaguar, coatimundi, weasels, raccoons, monkeys and others. Animals are released if and when they can survive in the wild... so you never know what animals you'll see here.

Children generally love animals, creating for them an amazing experience. However, these rescued animals may intimidate some young children. The sloth, for example, seems quite willing to sit in your lap so it would be a wonderful learning experience for them if they could brave the adventure. Like Jungla de Panamá, you might consider staying in one of Raquel's Ark's rental properties on site so you can wake up to exotic animals and get used to them gradually.

38. JARDIN ENCANTADO

Jardin Encantado lies hidden off Volcancito Road (the road to the west right before descending into Bajo Boquete. Translated as 'Charmed Garden' in English, this place is exactly that: a beautiful botanical garden complete with tropical birds and some exotic animals.

Claudia, the delightful German proprietor and chef, offers boutique guest rooms plus exquisite, multi-course fine dining by appointment only, and only for groups of 6 to 39. She believes in treating her guests like kings…and says that if a proprietor isn't willing to do that, he or she shouldn't be in the hospitality business. One thing is certain, Claudia has found her niche and is doing exactly what she wants to be doing.

Yes, among the beautiful flowers and plants, you'll find monkeys and macaws, even an ocelot, but think of this place as a delightful human 'respite and sanctuary' for those who can afford the regal treatment.

39. VOLCAN BARÚ

Boquete rests in a quiet valley divided by the Caldera River at the base of Volcan Barú, the tallest point in Panamá at 11,398 feet. While many consider the volcano dormant, technically it is not, according to the Institute of Geosciences at the University of Panamá. Scientists say Volcan Barú erupted around 1550 AD and last showed activity around 1600 AD. Their seismic equipment will give them several months' notice of any present danger.

Besides its looming presence around Boquete, Volcan Barú is known for being one place on earth where you can see both the Pacific Ocean and the Caribbean at the same time without binoculars. It should be on your bucket list to watch the sunrise from the top. Dozens attempt the climb every day, or rather every night at 11:00 p.m. they start off on a guided night hike to the summit hoping to arrive before the sun breaks through the clouds and lights up Boquete. It's a steep and rugged climb through rolling green hills, lush jungle and then rocky cliffs around the summit.

People consider this a 'once in a lifetime trek' – for the views to be sure – but also because the climb is not for the faint of heart or the weak-kneed. It takes experienced hikers often 5 to 6 hours to get from the ranger station to the top where they'll wait in freezing, pre-dawn wind gusts for the sun to arrive. Heading back down the hill is potentially even harder on your knees. If all goes well, you'll arrive back at your starting point about 11:30 a.m.

Not a big hiker? You can still experience the amazing sunrise and 'Pacific to the Caribbean' view by opting for a 4x4 Jeep Tour to the summit. Leaving at 4 a.m., the trek by Jeep only takes a couple hours and you'll be resting in a comfortable seat, with windows that close and protect you from the cold. But the road (if you want to call it that) is still gnarly, so consider it an extreme off-road experience. The jarring can be intense. The Jeep 4 x 4 Tour to Volcan

Barú isn't for people who are pregnant, have bad backs or have trouble with motion sickness.

40. CANOPY TOURS AND ZIP-LINING

Here's something else for your bucket list, albeit a friendlier, tamer adventure than going to the top of Volcan Barú to see the sunrise (unless you are afraid of heights.)

For centuries, people in different cultures have used different types of zip-lines to traverse both people and supplies across rivers and valleys. Still used by scientists and botanists studying jungles and remote areas, the enterprising idea of employing recreational zip-lines for ecotourism caught in the 1970s with everyday adventure seekers. Around Boquete, you have two options if you want to take a canopy tour and there's a third a bit farther away.

Tree Trek's safe canopy tour enjoys worldwide acclaim and you can take this 3.5 to 4 hour round trip excursion from Plaza Los Establos on Central Ave in downtown Boquete at three different times during the day. The tour itself includes 12 zip-line stations across about 2.75 miles bordering the National Park

La Amistad. You won't exactly float above the tops of century–old cloud forests, pristine rivers and waterfalls, because zip-lining requires a bit of muscular effort at times. But the scenery is amazing. I've not heard or seen the howler monkeys or the famed Quetzal while zip-lining, yet some have and you might.

A smaller 10-station zip-line attraction and 'Tarzan swing' can be found at Boquete Canopy Tours in the Bajo Mono area, on the road to the Lost Waterfalls Trail and Quetzal Trail.

Another place to zip-line is a little farther away, but if you base out of tranquil, cooler Boquete to visit the party area of Bocas del Toro, you might as well know your options. The Bastimentos Sky Zip-line Canopy Tour on the island hilltops of Isla Bastimentos, has a totally different, Caribbean vibe. The tour itself covers a much smaller area with only 7 tree-based stations but they have some other rope and play features that Tree Trek and Boquete Canopy Tours do not.

41. ARCHEOLOGICAL SITES & PETROGLYPHS

The chief motif on the southwest side of Chiriquí's Piedra Pintada de Caldera (Painted Stone of Caldera) resembles petroglyphs found in Puerto Rico, Venezuela and Colombia. No one knows for sure who did this work or what the purpose was. Researchers speculate the carvings to be more than 500 years old and possibly a vestige of the indigenous Doraces people long gone.

The Caldera boulders weigh several tons, and come from a super-explosion of Volcan Baru. Every part of the main boulder, especially the eastern side, is covered with figures but the markings are almost completely worn off the weathered side.

To get to Piedra Pintura from Boquete, stay on the main road through Caldera until you see a blue and white sign on the right side of the road indicating 'Los Petroglifos.' You can walk or even drive down the dirt/gravel road through the fence for about 380 yards until you find a group of rocks near a stream and small group of trees. Petroglyphs are on the largest rocks; the main rock has both petroglyphs and pictographs.

Please respect this treasure of Panamá. Do not mark the engravings with chalk, paint or any other substance 'to make them more visible.' It also goes without saying that it is inappropriate to deface the precious stone with your own initials, although some have. This interesting prehistoric rock is located in a farmer's field, and there is no admission charge or parking fee, but occasionally you may find the gate closed.

Sitio Barriles in Volcan, on the other hand, is one of the most famous archaeological sites in Panamá after National Geographic opened up the dig in 1949. If you are into early civilizations or truly unique energy fields, you'll want to check this place out. The property has been in the Landau-Haux family for generations and there is an admission fee to see the gardens, the stones and the outdoor 'museum.'

The petroglyphs were interesting and just what I expected to see. The magnetized stones, water flowing uphill, and the carvings that the guide said were from 1000 years before Christ, were not. These statues bear a strong resemblance to both Chinese and African peoples, whom our guide said were here long before even the Mayans, but scientists dispute this.

42. LOS LADRILLOS CLIMBING WALLS

Los Ladrillos means 'the bricks' or 'brickwork' in Spanish. On these natural basalt walls you can climb at the very beginner level to very advanced/difficult. In fact, Boquete is becoming an internationally known spot for rock climbing enthusiasts. I am not one of those enthusiasts, but the geographical formation is worth seeing anyway. It isn't difficult to get to or to park, and there are other good crags nearby as well.

Like most other places around here, if you don't have a car you can ask any taxi driver in Boquete to take you to "Los Ladrillos." It's well known. The wall is right off the road, being absolutely impossible to miss. The climbs range from about 55 ft. to close to 100 ft. Apparently you must have someone with you who can lead, because there is no top roping accessible without climbing the wall.

Boquete has a strong community of local climbers, so start a conversation with the ones you'll meet climbing at the wall and find out all about it. I always see people there when I go by. I'm told there's no need to bring your climbing gear with you. You can rent gear in town. Habla Ya offers daily rock

71

climbing tours, a multi-pitch rock climbing tour, and a hiking, climbing, rappelling circuit at Piedra de Lino Rock (see lesser known trails.)

43. THE PIPELINE TRAIL

The Pipeline Trail is a well-maintained, 'up-and-back' hike about 2.8 miles featuring gorgeous old-growth trees, abundant flora and fauna. You'll see the rusting pipeline for which the trail is named, cross a few bridges over a meandering creek and perhaps see a three-toed sloth or a resplendent quetzal. You do not need to take a guide as you can easily make this a self-guided hike, but a local guide can be helpful to explain the unique features of the area. You are likely to encounter more people taking doing this hike than Lost Waterfalls or Quetzal Trail because the Pipeline Trail is the easiest. Almost any one can do it. There is even a waterfall at the end of it, but it may be dry depending the time of year you go.

If you drive, you can park along the regular road near the intersection. Take the rutted gravel road by foot and walk just past the bend in the road. Beyond the bend you'll see a little building tucked under the pine trees and a gate. Someone will come out of the hut to collect your entrance fee.

44. THE LOST WATERFALLS TRAIL

The Lost Waterfalls path may be one of the most stunning jungle hikes in Panamá and possibly the entire world. You walk through the cloud forest to epic waterfalls where you can swim in crystal clear pools or explore a cave behind the one of the falls. If you are lucky, you might spot quetzals, sloths or even a tapir. You'll never forget the sound of howler monkeys if you hear them. This is an 'in and out' hike on private land, about 25 minutes outside Boquete, in the Bajo Mono area, the same area as Quetzal Trail and Pipeline Trail.

The consensus on these waterfalls is to skip the first one and to visit it on the way back. It's the largest, yet there's no real reason to see it last. For your safety, you can only admire it from the viewing platform. You can play in and explore the other waterfalls on this trail so maybe this is the reason to see them first. The third waterfall is the most strenuous to reach, so if 'physically demanding' is a problem for anyone in your group, you may want to skip that one and be satisfied with the jungle vines, bird sounds and general flora and fauna of the first two waterfalls.

To get to Lost Waterfalls Trails, catch a public bus, known as a 'Colectivo,' for a few bucks from the town square or consider a taxi, which might be cheaper if several people are going. If you drive, be prepared to pay a small parking fee. Once you get to the T in the intersection, a taxi stand will be on your right and several signs ahead of you, one pointing to Sendero Quetzales (Quetzales Trail) to the right and Lost Waterfalls. Turn right, go over the little bridge and act like you are going to Quetzal Trail. That trail starts when the road ends. Before you get to that point, you'll see a group of signs on your right for The Lost Waterfalls and for Sendero Culebra (Snake Path). Turn right there. Take the small suspension bridge across the river and follow the signs up the hill for about 10 minutes. You will reach a cabin where you pay the Lost Waterfalls entrance fee and sign the book so they can account for everyone at the end of the day.

To return to Boquete, you can call a taxi, wait for the next colectivo at the T (risky – they don't run on a regular basis) or flag down a passing motorist heading that way. This is common to share rides but you might find yourself in the open back of a truck.

45. THE QUETZALES TRAIL

I'm not a hardcore hiker but I love the outdoors. Some guidebooks say the Quetzal trail isn't that difficult, but it is. Its higher elevation and mud, combined with rickety handrails when they exist at all, make it treacherous in places. (An American actually slipped in December 2017 and died on the trail.) You are required to use a certified guide but they are still considering easing this restriction even with the 2017 accident. Taking a guide is a good idea regardless. He will have a machete and be able to help you through areas impacted by mudslides and fallen trees. He will also be quite familiar with the local flora and fauna. Some of it is poisonous; the guide will protect you.

The trail itself covers 7 km or about 4.35 miles. You can start at either end: Outside Cerro Punta on the other size of Volcan Barú, or outside Boquete, at the Alto Chiquero ranger station. At Alto Chiquero, the trail starts just as the road through the Bajo Mono area ends. At either end you'll pay a minimal amount to park your car and a park entrance fee. The trail is not 'in and out' like the Lost Waterfalls hike or the Pipeline trail, so you'd have to catch a ride back to your vehicle if you don't take a bus or taxi. Of course, you could just hike part way and turn around to return.

For that reason alone, if you aren't an avid hiker, aren't very physically fit or don't have Sendero Los Quetzales on your bucket list, you may choose not to hike it end to end. Having said that though, it is totally worth the time invested if you go. Be sure to take water, snacks, mosquito repellant and maybe a poncho for rain. You won't get a map so when you pay your entrance fee, take a photo of the large map with your cell phone and reference it later.

46. LESSER KNOWN TRAILS

White Rock (Peña Blanca) Trail is located near the Pipeline Trail in the Bajo Mono area within private land owned by the Landau family, one of Boquete's founding families. It's one of the easiest, flat hikes in Boquete and a good choice to get up close to wildlife like Resplendent Quetzal, sloths, howler monkeys and other wildlife. This trail is suitable for families with kids or people wanting less strenuous hikes.

Lino Rock (Piedra de Lino) is a short, yet steep, hike. Some will find it a challenge to reach the platform known as Lino Rock, but if you do, you'll be rewarded with one of the most stunning views of the Boquete valley. Rock climbers and rappellers play here. Most of the hike is through a typical coffee plantation and just the very last bit of it is through cloud forest.

The Fortress (La Artilleria) hike in the Alto Jaramillo area got its name from a legend saying the site was used to store weapons by local indigenous warriors. The trek is short and rewarding, offering you more fabulous views as it takes you through farmland, cloud forest and finally an impressive volcanic rock formation and cave. You'll even get a great view of the Pacific Ocean.

Mountain Lady (La Novia de la Montaña) is a short but challenging hike in the Horqueta region. It's called "the lady of the mountain" because you can see the face of a woman in the rocks - some say you can see many faces. The ceremonial altar in front of the waterfall makes you feel as if you're in a sacred place with ancient history. Tradition suggests that anyone who hikes in should go for a swim in the waterfall's pool. This trek is actually a favorite with birdwatchers because it takes you through an open space with trees on both sides. Perhaps you'll spot the famous Quetzal. The altitude on this trail only changes about 650 feet overall but some passages are quite steep.

The Pianist (El Pianista) Trail hike is one of the most overlooked excursions in Boquete. It's not marked well for tourists, although someone made some orange spray-painted markers on rocks and trees. The trail is located in the Rainbow (Arco Iris) section of Boquete, between Alto Lino and Palo Alto. It begins at the Il Pianista restaurant so if you don't see the hand-painted markers you can ask there. This trail used to be an important route all the way to Bocas del Toro across the Continental Divide. Hiking the whole trail it would take between 3 and 6 days, depending on your fitness and the weather. It is not recommended for children.

La Amistad - PILA (El Retoño y La Cascada). Parque Internacional La Amistad is an UNESCO World Heritage Site shared between Panama and Costa Rica, much it unmapped. Only 3% of PILA lies within the province of Chiriquí, but this part is the easiest to access. The park's plant and animal life are incredibly diverse. Start at the ranger station in the highlands of Cerro Punta to hike El Retoño, an easy 1.25 mile loop trail full of natural beauty. It's great for bird watching. This hike is fairly flat, taking you cloud forest, over small bridges across rushing streams and into a tunnel made from leaning stands of bamboo. From here you'll tackle La Cascada trail, a 2.5 mile hike that leads to a ridge with views of the valley and a spectacular waterfall.

Snake Trail or Sendero Culebra or is near the Lost Waterfalls trail. It's been used for centuries to go to Bocas del Toro but it would be much more challenging today since it is no longer maintained. Now it would take you anywhere from 5 to 7 days and should only be attempted in the dry season.

47. LOS CANGILÓNES DE GUALACA

Los Cangilones de Gualaca is a mini-canyon where it looks like the earth cracked, leaving a water trail below. The name means buckets or scoops. You can jump from the sides of the canyon into the blue water but the current can be quite strong. Some people climb the rocks back out but most just float down the canyon with the current and climb out of the river once it opens up. Then they walk a short distance back and do it all again.

Many people consider this spot better than a water park. Besides being gorgeous, this little gorge offers everything but public facilities. You'll want to pack drinks and snacks. In addition to cliff jumping (from lower and moderately high cliffs), swimming (shallow water in some areas for younger kids) and solo rock climbing, you can watch little fish and look for fossilized crustaceans. It's fairly exposed to the sun. The rocks heat up, so make sure you bring towels and something to lie on when you aren't in the water. Also use plenty of sunscreen.

By car from Boquete it takes about 40 minutes. Public transport is problematic because you would have to take a bus from Boquete to David then from

David to Gualaca, costing two hours of your life. An alternative is to go with a tour group through one of the adventure tour outfits in town. If there are several of you, perhaps you can get a good deal with a local taxi, which may end up being cheaper than a formal tour.

I highly recommend this out of the way place during the dry season. If you are here during the rainy season, you'll want to keep an eye on the locals. They say the river depth fluctuates between 13 and 26 feet. Heavy rains can rip through the canyon with little notice. Also, the water is more likely to be brown, not blue, during the rainy season.

My final recommendation regarding Los Cangilónes de Gualaca is to not come on the weekends. It can get really crowded and they charge a parking fee of several dollars on the weekends. However, whenever you do come, pack your trash up and take it with you. Some people leave trash behind because it's been a part of their culture, but this is changing in Panamá. Please contribute to maintaining this area's natural beauty rather than spoiling it.

48. CALDERA HOT SPRINGS

Like many 'must see' natural attractions around Boquete, these are not always well-marked and many are on private land. If you have a 4x4 you can drive to Caldera Hot Springs, except for a final 15-minute walk. The condition of the road really varies depending on ruts and mud. Alternatively, you can catch a bus from the main square in Boquete around 11 a.m. Be sure to ask the driver when the last pick up time is in Caldera, in order to return to Boquete. It is often 5 p.m.

From where the bus drops you off, the hot springs are at least another 45-60 minute walk. Go past the soccer field and you will see the Hot Springs sign on your right. The road takes you through cattle ranches and across an aqueduct. This sounds like a lot of walking until you realize that people do it all the time and the walk is gorgeous. Just remember to bring adequate water and some food with you.

The hot springs are small and natural. The water is around 104° F, heated by Volcan Barú. Besides a few pools you can go down to the river to swim. These 'back-to-basics' hot springs are not the biggest, the warmest or the nicest you may have ever enjoyed, but they stay popular and you can't beat the ambiance.

To go, once you pass the parking at the point of last return, you'll cross private land and someone from the house will come out and ask for a small fee per person. Don't feel like you are bothering anybody by being on private land. Social customs are different here. Collecting a small fee like this is common at these types of places throughout Latin America. This particular family has quite a few animals, including a monkey on a leash so just being there will likely seem quite out of the norm.

49. WHITE WATER RAFTING

Dry season or rainy season, there's a rafting trip for all skill levels in Chiriquí province. Spectacular scenery and passages through mysterious gorges in the middle of nowhere…you can find gentle rapids for families or churning water for hardcore rafters. In other words class II to class V rapids. If you're looking to experience the biggest whitewater in Central America, then as they say, the rivers of Panamá get even wilder during the rainy season, especially from June to November.

Several adventure tour groups in town offer rafting and kayaking.

Tours include air-conditioned transportation from Boquete to the rivers and back, and all gear including water shoes, helmet, paddle and life jacket. River water at the lower elevations is fairly warm due the location in the tropics. All you do is add the enthusiasm and the sunscreen.

Be sure to pay attention to the safety briefings… by personal experience I know it only takes one really good bounce to knock one out of the raft.

50. BEACH FUN FROM BOQUETE?

Unless you've been here before, who knew that Boquete makes a good base from which to go whale watching, surfing and snorkeling?

Great humpback whales migrate to Panamá from the south between mid-July and mid-October. A great way to view these magnificent animals is to take one of the guided whale-watching tours from Boquete. You'll leave the center of Boquete around 7 a.m. and ride in a comfortable, air-conditioned vehicle to Boca Chica, a small fishing village on the Pacific Coast east of David. There your group will board a boat that will take you out past the mangroves to the Gulf of Chiriquí National Marine Park. This large marine park/refuge consisting of about 25 uninhabited islands is truly gorgeous. Panamá set the area aside to provide protection for exotic fish, turtles, green iguanas and howler monkeys, among others. If you are lucky, you'll get catch glimpses of mama whales with their newborn calves and male whales breaching the surface. Tours include lunch, alcoholic and nonalcoholic drinks, use of snorkel equipment, hammocks, and beach towels...you just enjoy.

Speaking of snorkeling, we drove to Boca Chica on our own when my sister was visiting in March. The snorkeling tours were already full for the day we decided to go. But we had been told you could just go to Boca Chica and inquire with the locals to find someone who could take us out. We did this and to my surprise, it worked in no time at all. Our local guide even provided us with equipment. It was a gorgeous day and the ride out to the Gulf of Chiriquí National Marine Park was stunning. We saw a sea turtle dive as our boat approached.

Snorkeling in the Pacific does not compare with snorkeling in the Caribbean. On this excursion, we remained in fairly deep water and the waves were too much for my husband, who quickly became seasick. That forced us to head for a shallow bay within the refuge where he could recover on land and we could still play in the water seeing what we could see. The palm-treed island looked idyllic and the blue bay was certainly easier to snorkel in, but there wasn't much to see. To top it off, we were mildly and yet repeatedly stung by something in the water neither of us could see. The stings were mild and we suffered no ill affects after each momentary 'what was that?' contact.

You'll find much better snorkeling around Isla Bastimentos National Marine Park, Cayos Zapatilla, and Solarte Island (also known as Nancy's Cay) in the Bocas del Toro area of Panamá, on the Caribbean side of the mountains. It's just as close to Boquete 'as the crow flies.' Unfortunately with no direct route, driving takes about 4.5 hours, so plan on at least one overnight stay.

I had brought my snorkel gear with me when we moved to Panamá because my adopted home has thousands of miles of gorgeous beaches. I should have done more homework. Panamá is known as a surfer's paradise, and I don't happen to surf. But I have a 30-something friend of mine in Boquete who does. She tells me surfing is best in the Pacific between the months of April and November. There are several great places along the coast and coastal islands of Chiriquí for surfing, but some require special guides. For convenience, my friend usually heads to Las Lajas just east of David where she can surf any tide. Surfing there has a beach bottom break with rights and lefts but the waves are somewhat infrequent.

If surfing convenience isn't as important to you as finding ideal surf, then consider nearby Coiba Island,

Montuosa Island and La Barqueta Beach in Las Olas, where they hold surfing competitions.

TOP REASONS TO BOOK THIS TRIP

The weather in Boquete really is comfortable all year without any of the oppressive heat and humidity found in the rest of Panamá. So you can enjoy every aspect of your trip, whether you plan to hike and explore or kick back and relax. You'll fall in love with the eco-diversity, stunning views and friendly people... and likely find yourself dreaming of joining us, at least on a part-time basis.

A trip here whets your appetite and appreciation for the great outdoors in a unique and forever way, no matter what your age. Waterfalls and vistas seem to appear at every turn. As a biological gateway connecting the Americas, Boquete and the rest of Panamá sports some of the most exotic and diverse wildlife and plant habitats on the planet. I'm still surprised to see every houseplant I've ever nurtured in the States growing freely outside here, and much, much larger. Nothing compares to our volcanic soil, our cloud forests and our fresh, world-class coffee.

You'll find visiting Boquete is an easy and safe trip abroad, especially for first-timers. You don't need to calculate currency exchange rates or learn a new language, although knowing some Spanish would enhance your ability to fully appreciate this beautiful country.

Boquete is so much more than a bunch of active retirees living among pristine flowers. Backpackers and adventurists from the world over keep this a fascinating hamlet to visit or to call home. You'll meet the most interesting people here.

When and why you visit, or how long you'll stay, varies with each individual. However, those looking for both peace and adventure will all find one thing in common: It's so easy to become spoiled here.

"Live life with no excuses, travel with no regret"

– Oscar Wilde

BONUS BOOK

50 THINGS TO KNOW ABOUT PACKING LIGHT FOR TRAVEL

PACK THE RIGHT WAY EVERY TIME

AUTHOR: MANIDIPA BHATTACHARYYA

Edited by Melanie Howthorne

ABOUT THE AUTHOR

Manidipa Bhattacharyya is a creative writer and editor, with an
education in English literature and Linguistics. After working in the IT
industry for seven long years she decided to call it quits and follow her
heart instead. Manidipa has been ghost writing, editing, proof reading
and doing secondary research services for many story tellers and article
writers for about three years. She stays in Kolkata, India with her
husband and a busy two year old. In her own time Manidipa enjoys
travelling, photography and writing flash fiction.

Manidipa believes in travelling light and never carries anything that she
couldn't haul herself on a trip. However, travelling with her child
changed the scenario. She seemed to carry the entire world with her for
the baby on the first two trips. But good sense prevailed and she is
again working her way to becoming a light traveler, this time with a
kid.

INTRODUCTION

He who would travel happily
must travel light.

-Antoine de Saint-Exupéry

Travel takes you to different places from seas and mountains to deserts and much more. In your travels you get to interact with different people and their cultures. You will, however, enjoy the sights and interact positively with these new people even more, if you are travelling light.

When you travel light your mind can be free from worry about your belongings. You do not have to spend precious vacation time waiting for your luggage to arrive after a long flight. There is be no chance of your bags going missing and the best part is that you need not pay a fee for checked baggage.

People who have mastered this art of packing light will root for you to take only one carry-on, wherever you go. However, many people can find it really hard to pack light. More so if you are travelling with children. Differentiating between "must have" and "just in case" items is the starting point. There will be ample shopping avenues at your destination which are just waiting to be explored.

This book will show you 'packing' in a new 'light' –
pun intended – and help you to embrace light
packing practices for all of your future travels.

Off to packing!

DEDICATION

I dedicate this book to all the travel buffs that I know,
who have given me great insights into the contents of
their backpacks.

THE RIGHT TRAVEL GEAR

1. CHOOSE YOUR TRAVEL GEAR CAREFULLY

While selecting your travel gear, pick items that are
light weight, durable and most importantly, easy to
carry. There are cases with wheels so you can drag
them along – these are usually on the heavy side
because of the trolley. Alternatively a backpack that
you can carry comfortably on your back, or even a
duffel bag that you can carry easily by hand or sling
across your body are also great options. Whatever
you choose, one thing to keep in mind is that the
luggage itself should not weigh a ton, this will give
you the flexibility to bring along one extra pair of
shoes if you so desire.

2. CARRY THE MINIMUM NUMBER OF BAGS

Selecting light weight luggage is not everything. You need to restrict the number of bags you carry as well. One carry-on size bag is ideal for light travel. Most carriers allow one cabin baggage plus one purse, handbag or camera bag as long as it slides under the seat in front. So technically, you can carry two items of luggage without checking them in.

3. PACK ONE EXTRA BAG

Always pack one extra empty bag along with your essential items. This could be a very light weight duffel bag or even a sturdy tote bag which takes up minimal space. In the event that you end up buying a lot of souvenirs, you already have a handy bag to stuff all that into and do not have to spend time hunting for an appropriate bag.

I'm very strict with my packing and have everything in its right place. I never change a rule. I hardly use anything in the hotel room. I wheel my own wardrobe in and that's it.

Charlie Watts

95

CLOTHES & ACCESSORIES

4. PLAN AHEAD

Figure out in advance what you plan to do on your trip. That will help you to pick that one dress you need for the occasion. If you are going to attend a wedding then you have to carry formal wear. If not, you can ditch the gown for something lighter that will be comfortable during long walks or on the beach.

5. WEAR THAT JACKET

Remember that wearing items will not add extra luggage for your air travel. So wear that bulky jacket that you plan to carry for your trip. This saves space and can also help keep you warm during the chilly flight.

6. MIX AND MATCH

Carry clothes that can be interchangeably used to reinvent your look. Find one top that goes well with a couple of pairs of pants or skirts. Use tops, shirts and jackets wisely along with other accessories like a scarf or a stole to create a new look.

7. CHOOSE YOUR FABRIC WISELY

Stuffing clothes in cramped bags definitely takes its toll which results in wrinkles. It is best to carry wrinkle free, synthetic clothes or merino tops. This will eliminate the need for that small iron you usually bring along.

8. DITCH CLOTHES PACK UNDERWEAR

Pack more underwear and socks. These are the things that will give you a fresh feel even if you do not get a chance to wear fresh clothes. Moreover these are easy to wash and can be dried inside the hotel room itself.

9. CHOOSE DARK OVER LIGHT

While picking your clothes choose dark coloured ones. They are easy to colour coordinate and can last longer before needing a wash. Accidental food spills and dirt from the road are less visible on darker clothes.

10. WEAR YOUR JEANS

Take only one pair of Jeans with you, which you should wear on the flight. Remember to pick a pair that can be worn for sightseeing trips and is equally eloquent for dinner. You can add variety by adding light weight cargoes and chinos.

11. CARRY SMART ACCESSORIES

The right accessory can give you a fresh look even with the same old dress. An intelligent neck-piece, a couple of bright scarves, stoles or a sarong can be used in a number of ways to add variety to your clothing. These light weight beauties can double up as a nursing cover, a light blanket, beach wear, a modesty cover for visiting places of worship, and also makes for an enthralling game of peek-a-boo.

12. LEARN TO FOLD YOUR GARMENTS

Seasoned travellers all swear by rolling their clothes for compact and wrinkle free packing. Bundle packing, where you roll the clothes around a central object as if tying it up, is also a popular method of compact and wrinkle free packing. Stacking folded clothes one on top of another is a big no-no as it makes creases extreme and they are difficult to get rid of without ironing.

13. WASH YOUR DIRTY LAUNDRY

One of the ways to avoid carrying loads of clothes is to wash the clothes you carry. At some places you might get to use the laundry services or a Laundromat but if you are in a pinch, best solution is to wash them yourself. If that is the plan then carrying quick drying clothes is highly recommended, which most often also happen to be the wrinkle free variety.

14. LEAVE THOSE TOWELS BEHIND

Regular towels take up a lot of space, are heavy and take ages to dry out. If you are staying at hotels they will provide you with towels anyway. If you are travelling to a remote place, where the availability of towels look doubtful, carry a light weight travel towel of viscose material to do the job.

15. USE A COMPRESSION BAG

Compression bags are getting lots of recommendation now days from regular travellers. These are useful for saving space in your luggage when you have to pack bulky dresses. While packing for the return trip, get help from the hotel staff to arrange a vacuum cleaner.

FOOTWEAR

16. PUT ON YOUR HIKING BOOTS

If you have plans to go hiking or trekking during your trip, you will need those bulky hiking boots. The best way to carry them is to wear them on flight to save space and luggage weight. You can remove the boots once inside and be comfortable in your socks.

17. PICKING THE RIGHT SHOES

Shoes are often the bulkiest items, along with being the dainty if you are a female. They need care and take up a lot of space in your luggage. It is advisable therefore to pick shoes very carefully. If you plan to do a lot of walking and site seeing, then wearing a pair of comfortable walking shoes are a must. For more formal occasions you can carry durable, light weight flats which will not take up much space.

18. STUFF SHOES

If you happen to pack a pair of shoes, ensure you utilize their hollow insides. Tuck small items like rolled up socks or belts to save space. They will also be easy to find.

TOILETRIES

19. STASHING TOILETRIES

Carry only absolute necessities. Airline rules dictate
that for one carry-on bag, liquids and gels must be in
3.4 ounce (100ml) bottles or less, and must be packed
in a one quart zip-lock bag. If you are planning to stay
in a hotel, the basic things will be provided for you.
It's best is to buy the rest from the local market at
your destination.

20. TAKE ALONG TAMPONS

Tampons are a hard to find item in a lot of countries.
Figure out how many you need and pack accordingly.
For longer stays you can buy them online and have
them delivered to where you are staying.

21. GET PAMPERED BEFORE YOU TRAVEL

Some avid travellers suggest getting a pedicure and
manicure just the day before travelling. This not only
gives you a well kept look, you also save the trouble
of packing nail polish. Remember, every little bit of
weight reduced adds up.

ELECTRONICS

22. LUGGING ALONG ELECTRONICS

Electronics have a large role to play in our lives today. Most of us cannot imagine our lives away from our phones, laptops or tablets. However while travelling, one must consider the amount of weight these electronics add to our luggage. Thankfully smart phones come along with all the essentials tools like a camera, email access, picture editing tools and more. They are smart to the point of eliminating the need to carry multiple gadgets. Choose a smart phone that suits all your requirements and travel with the world in your palms or pocket.

23. REDUCE THE NUMBER OF CHARGERS

If you do travel with multiple electronic devices, you will have to bear the additional burden of carrying all their chargers too. Check if a single charger can be used for multiple devices. You might also consider investing in a pocket charger. These small devices support multiple devices while keeping you charged on the go.

24. TRAVEL FRIENDLY APPS

Along with smart phones come numerous apps, which are immensely helpful in our travels. You name it and you have an app for it at hand – take pictures, sharing with friends and family, torch to light dark roads, maps, checking flight/train times, find hotels and many other things. Use these smart alternatives to traditional items like books to eliminate weight and save space.

*I get ideas about what's essential
when packing my suitcase.*

-Diane von Furstenberg

TRAVELLING WITH KIDS

25. BRING ALONG THE STROLLER

Kids might enjoy walking for a while but they soon tire out and a stroller is the just the right thing for them to rest in while you continue your tour. Strollers also double duty as a luggage carrier and shopping bag holder. Remember to pick a light weight, easy to handle brand of stroller. Better yet, find out in advance if you can rent a stroller at your destination.

26. BRING ONLY ENOUGH DIAPERS FOR YOUR TRIP

Diapers take up a lot of space and add to the weight of your luggage. Therefore it is advisable to carry just enough diapers to last through the trip and a few for afterwards, till you buy fresh stock at your destination. Unless of course you are travelling to a really remote area, in which case you have no choice but to carry the load. Otherwise diapers are something you will find pretty easily.

27. TAKE ONLY A COUPLE OF TOYS

Children are easily attracted by new things in their environment. While travelling they will find numerous 'new' objects to scrutinize and play with. Packing just one favorite toy is enough, or if there is no favorite toy leave out all of them in favor of stories or imaginary games.

28. CARRY KID FRIENDLY SNACKS

Create a small snack counter in your bag to store away quick bites for those sudden hunger pangs. Depending on the child's age this could include chocolates, raisins, dry fruits, granola bars or biscuits. Also keep a bottle of water handy for your little one.

These things do not add much weight and can be adjusted in a handbag or knapsack.

29. GAMES TO CARRY

Create some travel specific, imaginary games if you have slightly grown up children, like spot the attractions. Keep a coloring book and colors handy for in-flight or hotel time. Apps on your smart phone can keep the children engaged with cartoons and story books. Older children are often entertained by games available on phones or tablets. This cuts the weight of luggage down while keeping the kids entertained.

30. LET THE KIDS CARRY THEIR LOAD

A good thing is to start early sharing of responsibilities. Let your child pick a bag of his or her choice and pack it themselves. Keep tabs on what they are stuffing in their bags by asking if they will be using that item on the trip. It could start out being just an entertainment bag initially but with growing years they will learn to sort the useful from the superfluous. Children as little as four can maneuver a small trolley suitcase like a pro- their experience in pull along toys credit. If you are worried that you may be pulling it for them, you may want to start with a backpack.

31. DECIDE ON LOCATION FOR CHILDREN TO SLEEP

While on a trip you might not always get a crib at your destination, and carrying one will make life all the more difficult. Instead call ahead to see if there are any cribs or roll out beds for children. You may even put blankets on the floor. Weave them a story about camping and they will gladly sleep without any trouble.

32. GET BABY PRODUCTS DELIVERED AT YOUR DESTINATION

If you are absolutely paranoid about not getting your favourite variety of diaper or brand of baby food, check out online stores like amazon.com for services in your destination city. You can buy things online ahead of your travel and get them delivered to your hotel upon arrival.

33. FEEDING NEEDS OF YOUR INFANTS

If you are travelling with a breastfed infant, you save the trouble of carrying bottles and bottle sanitization kits. For special food, or medications, you may need to call ahead to make sure you have a refrigerator where you are staying.

34. FEEDING NEEDS OF YOUR TODDLER

With the progression from infancy to toddler, their dietary requirements too evolve. You will have to pack some snacks for travelling time. Fresh fruits and vegetables can be purchased at your destination. Most of the cities you travel to in whichever part of the world, will have baby food products and formulas, available at the local drug-store or the supermarket.

35. PICKING CLOTHES FOR YOUR BABY

Contrary to popular belief, babies can do without many changes of clothes. At the most pack 2 outfits per day. Pack mix and match type clothes for your little one as well. Pick things which are comfortable to wear and quick to dry.

36. SELECTING SHOES FOR YOUR BABY

Like outfits, kids can make do with two pairs of comfortable shoes. If you can get some water resistant shoes it will be best. To expedite drying wet shoes, you can stuff newspaper in them then wrap them with newspaper and leave them to dry overnight.

37. KEEP ONE CHANGE OF CLOTHES HANDY

Travelling with kids can be tricky. Keep a change of clothes for the kids and mum handy in your purse or tote bag. This takes a bit of space in your hand luggage but comes extremely handy in case there are any accidents or spills.

38. LEAVE BEHIND BABY ACCESSORIES

Baby accessories like their bed, bath tub, car seat, crib etc. should be left at home. Many hotels provide a crib on request, while car seats can be borrowed from friends or rented. Babies can be given a bath in the hotel sink or even in the adult bath tub with a little bit of water. If you bring a few bath toys, they can be used in the bath, pool, and out of water. They can also be sanitized easily in the sink.

39. CARRY A SMALL LOAD OF PLASTIC BAGS

With children around there are chances of a number of soiled clothes and diapers. These plastic bags help to sort the dirt from the clean inside your big bag.

These are very light weight and come in handy to other carry stuff as well at times.

PACK WITH A PURPOSE

40. PACKING FOR BUSINESS TRIPS

One neutral-colored suit should suffice. It can be paired with different shirts, ties and accessories for different occasions. One pair of black suit pants could be worn with a matching jacket for the office or with a snazzy top for dinner.

41. PACKING FOR A CRUISE

Most cruises have formal dinners, and that formal dress usually takes up a lot of space. However you might find a tuxedo to rent. For women, a short black dress with multiple accessory options will do the trick.

42. PACKING FOR A LONG TRIP OVER DIFFERENT CLIMATES

The secret packing mantra for travel over multiple climates is layering. Layering traps air around your body creating insulation against the cold. The same light t-shirt that is comfortable in a warmer climate can be the innermost layer in a colder climate.

REDUCE SOME MORE WEIGHT

43. LEAVE PRECIOUS THINGS AT HOME

Things that you would hate to lose or get damaged leave them at home. Precious jewelry, expensive gadgets or dresses, could be anything. You will not require these on your trip. Leave them at home and spare the load on your mind.

44. SEND SOUVENIRS BY MAIL

If you have spent all your money on purchasing souvenirs, carrying them back in the same bag that you brought along would be difficult. Either pack everything in another bag and check it in the airport or get everything shipped to your home. Use an international carrier for a secure transit, but this could be more expensive than the checking fees at the airport.

45. AVOID CARRYING BOOKS

Books equal to weight. There are many reading apps which you can download on your smart phone or tab.

Plus there are gadgets like Kindle and Nook that are thinner and lighter alternatives to your regular book.

CHECK, GET, SET, CHECK AGAIN

46. STRATEGIZE BEFORE PACKING

Create a travel list and prepare all that you think you need to carry along. Keep everything on your bed or floor before packing and then think through once again – do I really need that? Any item that meets this question can be avoided. Remove whatever you don't really need and pack the rest.

47. TEST YOUR LUGGAGE

Once you have fully packed for the trip take a test trip with your luggage. Take your bags and go to town for window shopping for an hour. If you enjoy your hour long trip it is good to go, if not, go home and reduce the load some more. Repeat this test till you hit the right weight.

48. ADD A ROLL OF DUCT TAPE

You might wonder why, when this book has been talking about reducing stuff, we're suddenly asking you to pack something totally unusual. This is because when you have limited supplies, duct tape is immensely helpful for small repairs – a broken bag, leaking zip-lock bag, broken sunglasses, you name it and duct tape can fix it, temporarily.

49. LIST OF ESSENTIAL ITEMS

Even though the emphasis is on packing light, there are things which have to be carried for any trip. Here is our list of essentials:

•Passport/Visa or any other ID

•Any other paper work that might be required on a trip like permits, hotel reservation confirmations etc.

•Medicines – all your prescription medicines and emergency kit, especially if you are travelling with children

•Medical or vaccination records

•Money in foreign currency if travelling to a different country

•Tickets- Email or Message them to your phone

50. MAKE THE MOST OF YOUR TRIP

Wherever you are going, whatever you hope to do we encourage you to embrace it whole-heartedly. Take in the scenery, the culture and above all, enjoy your time away from home.

On a long journey even a straw weighs heavy.

-Spanish Proverb

PACKING AND PLANNING TIPS

A Week before Leaving

- Arrange for someone to take care of pets and water plants.

- Stop mail and newspaper.

- Notify Credit Card companies where you are going.

- Change your thermostat settings.

- Car inspected, oil is changed, and tires have the correct pressure.

- Passports and photo identification is up to date.

- Pay bills.

- Copy important items and download travel Apps.

- Start collecting small bills for tips.

Right Before Leaving

- Clean out refrigerator.

- Empty garbage cans.

- Lock windows.

- Make sure you have the proper identification with you.

- Bring cash for tips.

- Remember travel documents.

- Lock door behind you.

- Remember wallet.

- Unplug items in house and pack chargers.

>TOURIST

READ OTHER
GREATER THAN A TOURIST
BOOKS

Greater Than a Tourist San Miguel de Allende Guanajuato Mexico:
50 Travel Tips from a Local by Tom Peterson

Greater Than a Tourist – Lake George Area New York USA:
50 Travel Tips from a Local by Janine Hirschklau

Greater Than a Tourist – Monterey California United States:
50 Travel Tips from a Local by Katie Begley

Greater Than a Tourist – Chanai Crete Greece:
50 Travel Tips from a Local by Dimitra Papagrigoraki

Greater Than a Tourist – The Garden Route Western Cape Province
South Africa: 50 Travel Tips from a Local by Li-Anne McGregor van
Aardt

Greater Than a Tourist – Sevilla Andalusia Spain:
50 Travel Tips from a Local by Gabi Gazon

Greater Than a Tourist – Kota Bharu Kelantan Malaysia:
50 Travel Tips from a Local by Aditi Shukla

Children's Book: Charlie the Cavalier Travels the World by Lisa
Rusczyk

>TOURIST

> TOURIST

Visit Greater Than a Tourist for Free Travel Tips
http://GreaterThanATourist.com

Sign up for the Greater Than a Tourist Newsletter for
discount days, new books, and travel information:
http://eepurl.com/cxspyf

Follow us on Facebook for tips, images, and ideas:
https://www.facebook.com/GreaterThanATourist

Follow us on Pinterest for travel tips and ideas:
http://pinterest.com/GreaterThanATourist

Follow us on Instagram for beautiful travel images:
http://Instagram.com/GreaterThanATourist

>TOURIST

> TOURIST

Please leave your honest review of this book on Amazon and Goodreads. Please send your feedback to GreaterThanaTourist@gmail.com as we continue to improve the series. We appreciate your positive and constructive feedback. Thank you.

METRIC CONVERSIONS

TEMPERATURE

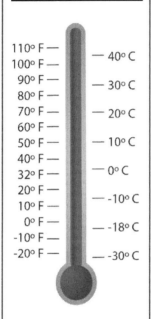

110° F — — 40° C
100° F —
90° F — — 30° C
80° F —
70° F — — 20° C
60° F —
50° F — — 10° C
40° F —
32° F — — 0° C
20° F —
10° F — — -10° C
0° F — — -18° C
-10° F —
-20° F — — -30° C

To convert F to C:

Subtract 32, and then multiply
by 5/9 or .5555.

To Convert C to F:

Multiply by 1.8
and then add 32.

32F = 0C

LIQUID VOLUME

To Convert:................Multiply by
U.S. Gallons to Liters............... 3.8
U.S. Liters to Gallons 26
Imperial Gallons to U.S. Gallons 1.2
Imperial Gallons to Liters....... 4.55
Liters to Imperial Gallons 22

1 Liter = .26 U.S. Gallon
1 U.S. Gallon = 3.8 Liters

DISTANCE

To convert ....Multiply by
Inches to Centimeters 2.54
Centimeters to Inches 39
Feet to Meters...................... .3
Meters to Feet 3.28
Yards to Meters 91
Meters to Yards 1.09
Miles to Kilometers 1.61
Kilometers to Miles............ .62
1 Mile = 1.6 km
1 km = .62 Miles

WEIGHT

1 Ounce = .28 Grams
1 Pound = .4555 Kilograms
1 Gram = .04 Ounce
1 Kilogram = 2.2 Pounds

TRAVEL QUESTIONS

- Do you bring presents home to family or friends after a vacation?

- Do you get motion sick?

- Do you have a favorite billboard?

- Do you know what to do if there is a flat tire?

- Do you like a sun roof open?

- Do you like to eat in the car?

- Do you like to wear sun glasses in the car?

- Do you like toppings on your ice cream?

- Do you use public bathrooms?

- Did you bring your cell phone and does it have power?

- Do you have a form of identification with you?

- Have you ever been pulled over by a cop?

- Have you ever given money to a stranger on a road trip?

- Have you ever taken a road trip with animals?

- Have you ever went on a vacation alone?

- Have you ever run out of gas?

- If you could move to any place in the world, where would it be?

- If you could travel anywhere in the world, where would you travel?

- If you could travel in any vehicle, which one would it be?

- If you had three things to wish for from a magic genie, what would they be?

- If you have a driver's license, how many times did it take you to pass the test?

- What are you the most afraid of on vacation?

- What do you want to get away from the most when you are on vacation?

- What foods smells bad to you?

- What item do you bring on ever trip with you away from home?

- What makes you sleepy?

- What song would you love to hear on the radio when you're cruising on the highway?

- What travel job would you want the least?

- What will you miss most while you are away from home?

- What is something you always wanted to try?

- What is the best road side attraction that you ever saw?

- What is the farthest distance you ever biked?

- What is the farthest distance you ever walked?

- What is the weirdest thing you needed to buy while on vacation?

- What is your favorite candy?

- What is your favorite color car?

- What is your favorite family vacation?

- What is your favorite food?

- What is your favorite gas station drink or food?

- What is your favorite license plate design?

- What is your favorite restaurant?

- What is your favorite smell?

- What is your favorite song?

- What is your favorite sound that nature makes?

- What is your favorite thing to bring home from a vacation?

- What is your favorite vacation with friends?

- What is your favorite way to relax?

- Where is the farthest place you ever traveled in a car?

- Where is the farthest place you ever went North, South, East and West?

- Where is your favorite place in the world?

- Who is your favorite singer?

- Who taught you how to drive?

- Who will you miss the most while you are away?

- Who if the first person you will contact when you get to your destination?

- Who brought you on your first vacation?

- Who likes to travel the most in your life?

- Would you rather be hot or cold?

- Would you rather drive above, below, or at the speed limited?

- Would you rather drive on a highway or a back road?

- Would you rather go on a train or a boat?

- Would you rather go to the beach or the woods?

TRAVEL BUCKET LIST

1.

2.

3.

4.

5.

6.

7.

8.

9.

10.

NOTES

Made in the USA
Columbia, SC
27 August 2019